Contents

T0313578

Written by
David Grant

Illustrated by
Nelson Evergreen

Series editor **Dee Reid**

ALWAYS LEARNING

PEARSON

Before reading *Stone Cold Dead*

Characters

Jamie Hill

Jamie's dad

The old lady

New vocabulary

ch1 p6 shuffled
ch2 p10 derelict
ch3 p13 gasped

ch3 p15 grimly
ch4 p18 frantically
ch4 p19 definitely

Introduction

Hill Hall was where Jamie's family used to live a long time ago, so Jamie and his dad visit it to find out more about their family tree. Hill Hall is now a hotel run by a creepy old lady and it turns out she knows a few facts about Jamie's family tree.

Stone Cold Dead

Chapter One

An elderly lady waited by the entrance of
Hill Hall Hotel on the lookout for her guests.
It was nearly dark when she heard a loud knock
at the door. She carefully opened the creaking
door and saw a man and a boy standing on
the doorstep.

"You must be Edward Hill," said the old lady, "and I am guessing this is your son, Jamie."

The man nodded.

"Welcome," she said. "I'll show you to your room."

Their room was large and gloomy.

"The Hill family used to live here a long time ago, didn't they?" asked Jamie.

"Yes… they did," said the old lady.

"My family are called Hill," said Jamie. "We've come to find out about the Hill family tree."

"Do you know anything about the Hill family?"
Dad asked her.

"Oh yes," she said and gave an odd smile. Jamie
felt the hairs rise on the back of his neck.

"Sleep well," said the old lady as she shuffled
out of the room.

Chapter Two

In the middle of the night Jamie suddenly woke up.

He had heard a noise. It sounded like someone

scratching their nails on the window.

"Dad, listen to that scratching sound!" whispered

Jamie.

Dad went to the window. He saw the old lady standing in the garden.

"What on earth is going on?" he called down to her.

She didn't answer. She just waved at them to come down and follow her. They grabbed some clothes and ran outside. But when they got outside, the old lady had disappeared.

"Where is she?" said Dad, looking around wildly. "I can't see her."

"There she is!" yelled Jamie, pointing towards a lake in the hotel grounds.

The old lady was standing on the path by the lake, waving at them to follow her. Jamie and his dad set off for the lake. But when they searched near the lake there was no sign of the old lady.

"Now where has she gone?" asked Jamie's dad.

"She's over there! By the trees!" said Jamie.

They saw her stop by a derelict stone shed and then go inside. Jamie and his dad followed her. The shed was very cold and damp, with just one little window.

"What's going on?" demanded Jamie's dad.

"I have brought you here to tell you a story," said the old lady. Again she gave a strange smile. Jamie shivered.

Chapter Three

"I'm going to tell you a story about someone from your family," said the old lady. "Almost two hundred years ago on an icy cold night just like tonight, a man called Edward Hill planned to meet a girl who worked in the Hall. They were to meet in this shed."

"Her name was Mary Hinton," said the
old lady. "Edward tried to kiss her. But
Mary did not want to kiss him. He was
so angry that he locked her in this shed on that
cold night. By the morning, she had died from
the cold."

"That's terrible," gasped Jamie.

"Look!" said the old lady as she gazed out of the

little window. "It's started to snow."

"We must insist on going back to the hotel now,

we are really cold," said Jamie's dad.

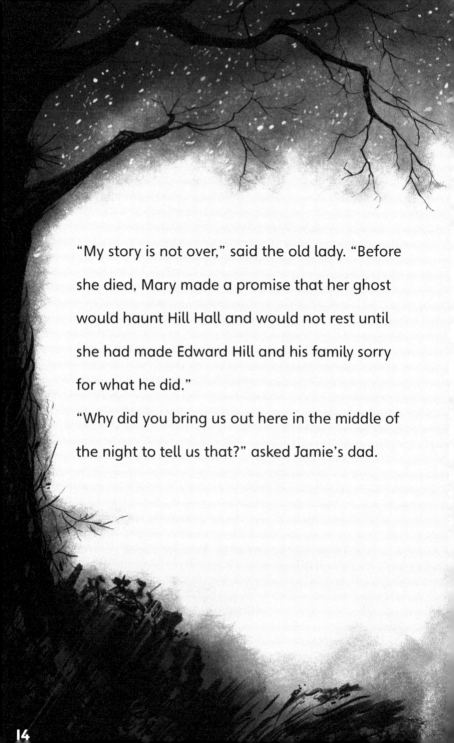

"My story is not over," said the old lady. "Before she died, Mary made a promise that her ghost would haunt Hill Hall and would not rest until she had made Edward Hill and his family sorry for what he did."

"Why did you bring us out here in the middle of the night to tell us that?" asked Jamie's dad.

"Because your name is Edward Hill," said the old lady grimly as she pointed a finger at him. "And my name is Mary Hinton."

Jamie's dad went white and his mouth dropped open. "But you're mad," he shouted. "I'm not the same Edward Hill!"

"I don't care," snapped the old lady, "you are still Edward Hill's family."

Jamie stared in horror at the crazy old lady. Suddenly she did not look the same. Her hair was not grey, it was darker. Her skin was not pale, it was brighter. She looked like a young woman. And then she faded until Jamie could see right through her. As she walked out of the door, it banged shut behind her.

Jamie let out a scream of fear. His dad tried to pull open the door but it was already locked from the outside.

They both tried as hard as they could to kick the door down but they couldn't. Next Jamie tried to escape through the little window. His dad tried to push him through the gap but Jamie was too big. They stood in the darkness, looking through the dusty little window at the snow.

Chapter Four

"Quick, Jamie, have you got your phone?" said his dad.

Jamie felt in his pocket. "It's in the hotel room," he said.

"Mine too," said his dad. He groaned and frantically kicked the door again.

"I'm freezing!" said Jamie shaking with cold.

"Me too," said Dad.

Jamie began to cry.

"Help!" shouted Jamie's dad at the top of his

voice. Nothing happened. No one answered.

"We'll have to stay here until the morning,"

said Jamie's dad quietly. "I'm sure someone will

definitely rescue us then."

They sat down on the ice-cold stone floor to wait.

Hours went by. It was getting colder. After a while

they slipped into sleep.

The next morning, the old lady came out of the front door of Hill Hall Hotel. She thought of Jamie and his dad in the cold stone shed. "Stone cold dead," she said to herself – and she smiled. She looked up at Hill Hall Hotel. It looked like no one had lived in the building for years.

She locked the door and walked through the snow to the gate. When she reached the gate, she locked it. She looked back and noticed there were no footprints in the snow. As she looked, she started fading. She slowly faded until she disappeared.

Quiz

p5 Why did Jamie and his dad visit Hill Hall Hotel?
a) To have a meal.
b) To find out about their family tree.
c) They liked the look of the hotel.

p10 Why did the old lady make Jamie and his dad follow her to the stone shed?
a) To give them tea.
b) To play a game.
c) To tell them a story.

p12 Why was the first Edward Hill angry?
a) Mary would not kiss him.
b) He had lost the key to the shed.
c) It was icy cold.

p12 What happened to Mary after she was locked in the shed?
a) She was rescued.
b) She climbed out of the window.
c) She died from the cold.

p17 Why couldn't Jamie and his dad escape out of the window?
a) It was too dusty.
b) It was snowing.
c) The window was too small.

Inferential comprehension

- What clues are there that the old lady is glad Jamie and his dad visited Hill Hall Hotel?

- How do we know that Jamie found the old lady creepy?

- How can we tell that Jamie's dad is cross with the old lady?

- What evidence is there that Mary Hinton was a ghost?

- Why does the title of the story suit the plot?

Personal response

- Would you have followed the old lady when she waved from the garden?

- How would you have felt if you were Jamie and his dad stuck in the ice-cold shed?

- Do you think people can come back from the dead to haunt people?

- Do you think it was fair that Jamie and his dad were killed for something their relative did a long time ago?

Published by Pearson Education Limited, Edinburgh Gate, Harlow, Essex, CM20 2JE.

www.pearsonschoolsandfecolleges.co.uk

Text © Pearson Education Limited 2012

Edited by Bethan Phillips
Designed by Siu Hang Wong
Original illustrations © Pearson Education Limited 2012
Illustrated by Nelson Evergreen
Cover design by Siu Hang Wong
Cover illustration © Pearson Education Limited 2012

The right of David Grant to be identified as author of this work has been asserted by him in
accordance with the Copyright, Designs and Patents Act 1988.

First published 2012

21
13

British Library Cataloguing in Publication Data
A catalogue record for this book is available from the British Library

ISBN 978 0 435 07164 6

Printed in Great Britain by Ashford Colour Press Ltd